True Stories From Ancient China

Distinguished Doctors
and Miraculous Remedies

By Zhu Kang

Illustrated by Hong Tao and Feng Congying

LONG RIVER PRESS
San Francisco

Copyright © 2005 Long River Press

Published in the United States of America by

LONG RIVER PRESS
360 Swift Avenue, Suite 48
South San Francisco, CA 94080
www.longriverpress.com

In association with Dolphin Books

Editor: Luo Tianyou

No part of this book may be reproduced without written permission of the Publisher.

ISBN 1-59265-036-8

Library of Congress Control Number: 2004113546

Printed in China

10 9 8 7 6 5 4 3 2 1

BIAN QUE AND THE
FOUR METHODS OF DIAGNOSIS

扁鹊

QIN YUEREN (401-314 B.C.) WAS ONE OF THE
FOUNDERS OF TRADITIONAL CHINESE MEDICINE. HE
IS BEST KNOWN FOR HIS SYSTEMATIC APPROACH TO
DIAGNOSIS, ALSO KNOWN AS THE FOUR METHODS:
TO OBSERVE; TO LISTEN; TO ASK; TO FEEL

IN ANCIENT TIMES, PEOPLE PLACED THEIR FAITH IN DIVINATION, SUCH AS GODS, GHOSTS, AND DIETIES RATHER THAN IN DOCTORS. WHENEVER AN EPIDEMIC OR OUTBREAK OF DISEASE OCCURRED, CEREMONIAL RITES WERE PERFORMED AND PEOPLE PRAYED TO THE GODS FOR THEIR SAFETY.

WHEN HE WAS YOUNG, QIN YUEREN WORKED BY DOING ODD JOBS AT AN INN

Qin! What are you staring at? Get back to work!

Ten days have passed and yet the deaths continue from this strange disease.

Why can't the plague be dispelled?

Alas!

If any more people are infected, it will be the end of my business!

I feel weak all over.

He has no one to turn to for help. Where should he go?

Let me have a look.

CHANG SANG WAS AN OLD FOLK DOCTOR

Now, follow this prescription and you'll be alright.

2

Zhao Jianzi, a great officer of the state of Jin, is critically ill. I was sent here to collect you. He needs your treatment!

He has been unconscious for five days!

Although his pulse is weak, he can still be saved. Help me, Madam!

You're awake!

Master Qin! You truly are a reincarnation of Bian Que!

BIAN QUE WAS A LEGENDARY MAGICAL BIRD THAT COULD CURE DISEASE. FROM THIS MOMENT ON, QIN YUEREN WAS KNOWN AS BIAN QUE.

AT THAT TIME, CHINA WAS DIVIDED INTO MANY KINGDOMS. BIAN QUE, TOGETHER WITH HIS APPRENTICE, PRACTICED MEDICINE WHEREVER HE COULD AND HIS FAME SPREAD FAR AND WIDE. ONE DAY AN ENVOY FROM THE STATE OF QIN VISITED HIM.

Our King knows your reputation and he invites you to the palace. Come with me.

Fascinating! Your experiences are truly amazing. Tell me more.

Yes, Lord.

If I may speak, Sire, I see that you have a disease hidden under your skin. It should be treated immediately.

Oh come now! Do you mean to say you can see under my skin? Good day, Sir!

Doctors like Bian Que think that even a healthy man like me is a patient.

Long live His Majesty!

6

A FEW DAYS LATER.

My Lord, I see that your disease has spread to your blood. If not treated now, it'll only get worse.

I'm quite well. Good day, Sir!

Sire! Your disease is spreading! It will soon become very dangerous!

Why is Bian Que so animated? What if—what if he is right?

I will speak to him, Majesty.

What can you tell me about His Majesty's condition?

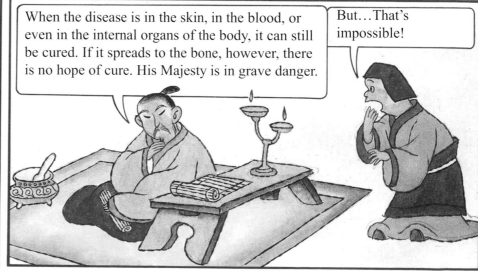

When the disease is in the skin, in the blood, or even in the internal organs of the body, it can still be cured. If it spreads to the bone, however, there is no hope of cure. His Majesty is in grave danger.

But...That's impossible!

Master, why are you packing your things?

(Sigh). His Majesty has refused treatment. We may as well take our leave.

LATER, THEY RECEIVED NEWS OF THE KING'S DEATH.

Before he died, His Majesty regretted that he hadn't taken your advice.

Alas, it is too late.

A FEW DAYS LATER, BIAN QUE ARRIVED IN THE STATE OF WEI.

Master, what are they all talking about?

9

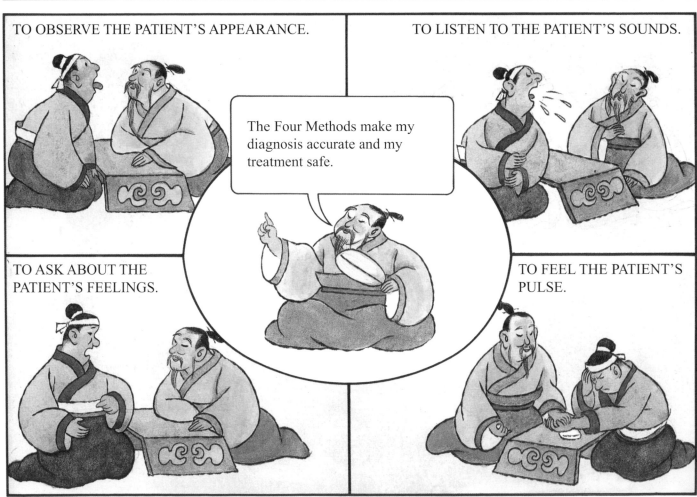

FOR YEARS, BIAN QUE TRAVELED THE COUNTRYSIDE PRACTICING MEDICINE, EVEN AFTER HE HAD REACHED THE AGE OF 80.

Doctor Li, bring Bian Que to see me as soon as he arrives.

Yes, Sir.

What's the matter, Doctor?

His Majesty wants Bian Que! I'll never become the imperial physician!

Oh, is *that* all? Just leave it to me. We'll take care of Bian Que.

Be careful!

Who's there?

A child is dying! Please save him, Bian Que!

I'm coming. Up quickly, all of you!

11

Where is the...

AS A RESULT OF TRETCHERY, BIAN QUE WAS ASSASINATED. HIS NINE PUPILS, HOWEVER, CARRIED ON HIS TEACHINGS.

BIAN QUE ADVOCATED TREATING ONLY THOSE WHO WERE NOT SELF-INDULGENT, GREEDY, IRRESPONSIBLE, WEAK IN MORAL CHARACTER, AND THOSE WHO BELIEVED IN SORCERY. ONLY WHEN THESE NEGATIVE TRAITS WERE OVERCOME COULD THE PEOPLE TRULY BENEFIT FROM MEDICAL CARE.

BY THE HAN DYNASTY, BIAN QUE'S MEDICAL THEORIES AND EXPERIENCES WERE SUMMED UP IN A CLASSIC MEDICINAL TEXT ENTITLED "THE YELLOW EMPEROR'S CLASSIC ON 81 MEDICAL PROBLEMS," WHICH EXERTED A GREAT INFLUENCE ON THE DEVELOPMENT OF MEDICAL SCIENCE IN CHINA FOR FUTURE GENERATIONS.

HUA TUO AND THE FIVE-ANIMAL EXERCISES

华佗

A DISTINGUSHED DOCTOR OF ANCIENT CHINA, HUA TUO (145-208 A.D.) MADE REMARKABLE ACHIEVEMENTS IN THE DIAGNOSIS OF DISEASE, AS WELL AS BEING THE FIRST DOCTOR IN CHINA TO CONDUCT SURGERY USING ANAESTHESIA.

Look at General Guan! He is really a hero. He is playing chess even while Hua Tuo is cutting him with a knife!

The General is cured once Hua Tuo is finished. He is truly the world's greatest doctor.

IN THE SECOND CENTURY A.D., GUAN YU, A FAMOUS GENERAL OF THE STATE OF SHU, WAS WOUNDED BY A POISONED ARROW. HE SUMMONED HUA TUO TO HIS CAMP.

MOST PATIENTS, HOWEVER, WERE NOT AS BRAVE AS THE GENERAL.

Let's get out of here! I'd rather die than be in that much pain!

He's fainted from the pain!

Clean the wound and dress it immediately.

I must find a solution. No one can stand the pain of an operation.

IN ANCIENT TIMES, DOCTORS WERE RESPONSIBLE FOR PLANTING AND COLLECTING MEDICINAL HERBS.

Master! Don't eat that! It might be poisonous!

There must be an herbal solution.

Let's ask the woodcutters living in the mountains. Perhaps they know these plants.

Oh! The pain! The pain!

Oww!

Are you a doctor? Please save my husband!

He is always hungry, but he can't swallow anything due to the pain in his throat.

I will.

Mix three bowls of vinegar with mashed garlic. Make him drink it.

15

We're almost there.

Please give me three bowls of vinegar with mashed garlic.

Very well.

Oh My! Look! A huge roundworm!

You're lucky to have met Hua Tuo. He truly is a magic doctor!

Food and wine for everyone! When I'm done, I'll go thank Hua Tuo.

Coming up!

Hua Tuo! Look at this roundworm I had inside me! I can eat meat now.

Thank you for saving my life.

If you eat clean food in the future, the roundworm won't grow in your body anymore.

Why are you collecting that plant, Doctor?

This is *Datura*. This man told me it functions like an anesthetic.

I've heard bandits use it to drug their victims before robbing them!

"?"

"?"

Collect as many leaves as you can!

OK!

Now, we need to add several more herbs to detoxify the Datura, so the anesthetic will be safe.

17

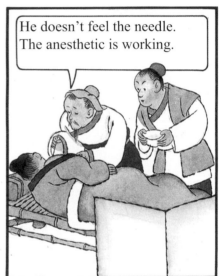

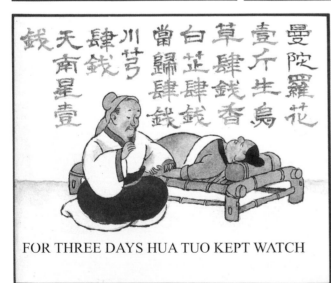

FOR THREE DAYS HUA TUO KEPT WATCH

HUA TUO INVENTED *MA FEI SAN* (AN EARLY FORM OF MORPHINE). AFTERWARD, HE WAS ABLE TO PERFORM SURGERY. WHILE THIS OCCURRED OVER 1,700 YEARS AGO, WESTERN ANESTHESIA HAS BEEN USED FOR ONLY A FRACTION OF THAT TIME.

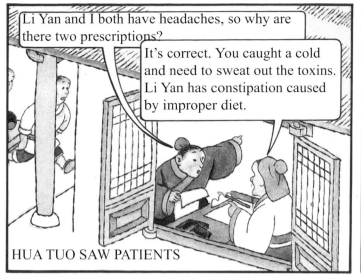

Li Yan and I both have headaches, so why are there two prescriptions?

It's correct. You caught a cold and need to sweat out the toxins. Li Yan has constipation caused by improper diet.

HUA TUO SAW PATIENTS

My brother has a stomach ache. Can you see him please?

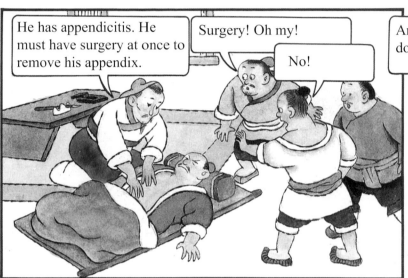

He has appendicitis. He must have surgery at once to remove his appendix.

Surgery! Oh my!

No!

Argh! I can't bear the pain! Quickly, doctor!

Give him *mafeisan* at once and prepare him for surgery!

LATER, HUA TUO SUCCESSFULLY REMOVED THE MAN'S APPENDIX

When he wakes up, he'll be in pain. Give him these medicinal herbs and he'll be fine.

19

Doctor! You saved my life!

Let me have a look at you.

It's healing well? Now I can go to work again.

He was lucky to have your care. What can I do to stay healthy?

Remember to exercise frequently. I'm going to the mountains to collect wild herbs. Care to join me?

Sure.

HUA TUO OFTEN WENT TO THE MOUNTAINS TO COLLECT MEDICINAL HERBS

Master! Look! A tiger! Stay still!

I think the tiger has gone.

Hmm. If a person can be strong like a tiger, he won't get sick.

Yeah! If you run and jump like a tiger and eat raw meat for a year!

You speak the truth. If we humans can follow the movements and actions of animals, we can improve our overall health.

HUA TUO INVENTED THE FIVE-ANIMAL EXERCISES TO IMITATE THE MOVEMENT OF THE TIGER, DEER, BEAR, MONKEY, AND FALCON.

HUA TUO'S FAME GREW. SOON, HE WAS SUMMONED TO APPEAR BEFORE CAO CAO, THE PRIME MINISTER OF THE STATE OF WEI.

HUA TUO ORGANIZED GROUP PARTICIPATION IN THE FIVE-ANIMAL EXERCISES, ONE OF THE FIRST SUCH ACTIVITIES IN CHINESE HISTORY.

I'd like to go out and visit the countryside.

Impossible! The Imperial Doctor never leaves the palace!

We're like birds in a cage, Master.

We'll say we need to collect medicinal herbs.

HUA TUO GREW TIRED OF PALACE LIFE. BY TELLING EVERYONE HIS WIFE WAS ILL, HE WAS GRANTED A LEAVE OF ABSENCE TO RETURN HOME.

My head is hurting again! Hua Tuo has been gone too long. Summon him back to the palace!

He said his wife was seriously ill and asked to extend his leave.

CAO CAO'S PATIENCE GREW THIN.

Go to Hua Tuo's home to see if his wife is really ill. If she is not, bring him to me at once!

Hua Tuo! You dare to deceive our Master? We know your wife is not ill. You are to come with us immediately!

Don't worry my dear. I'll be back soon.

If you want to be rid of your headache once and for all, I must operate.

24

IMPRISONED, HUA TUO MADE A RECORD OF ALL HIS KNOWLEDGE

HUA TUO BURNED HIS WRITINGS BEFORE DYING IN PRISON.
HIS MEDICINAL TEXTS WERE LOST FOREVER.

WANG WEIYI AND THE BRONZE STATUE

王惟一

BORN IN 987, WANG WEIYI WAS A DOCTOR IN THE SONG DYNASTY. HE WAS THE FIRST TO CAST BRONZE MODELS OF THE HUMAN BODY INSCRIBED WITH ACUPUNCTURE POINTS. WANG MADE GREAT CONTRIBUTIONS TO THE FIELD OF TRADITIONAL CHINESE MEDICINE.

TRADITIONAL CHINESE MEDICINE WAS COMPRISED OF MANY FORMS.

ACUPUNCTURE THERAPY WAS TO INSERT A SILVER NEEDLE IN A CERTAIN LOCATION OF THE MERIDIAN: TWISTING, TURNING, AND LIFTING THE NEEDLE TO CLEAR THE BODY'S PATHWAY.

MOXIBUSTION THERAPY INVOLVED CLEARING IMPURITIES FROM THE BODY BY USING HEATED AIR CONCENTRATED IN A NARROW TUBE.

TOGETHER, ACUPUNCTURE AND MOXIBUSTION HAVE A HISTORY OF MORE THAN 2,500 YEARS IN CHINA.

I feel much better!

TRADITIONAL CHINESE MEDICINE HELD THAT MERIDIANS AND COLLATERALS WERE PATHWAYS OF THE BODY IN WHICH BLOOD AND QI (VITAL ENERGY) CONSTANTLY CIRCULATED. THEY FORMED A NETWORK IN WHICH THE TISSUES AND ORGANS OF THE BODY WERE LINKED AS AN ORGANIC WHOLE. WHEN THE FLOW WAS IMPEDED, A PERSON WOULD BECOME ILL.

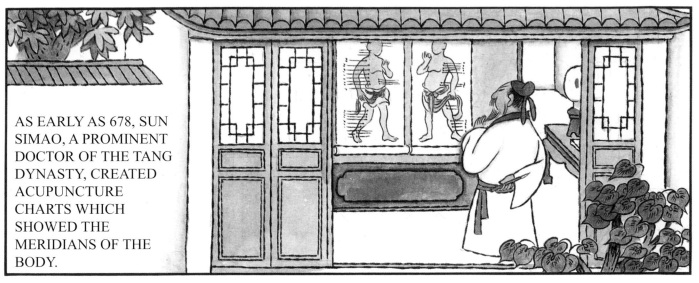

AS EARLY AS 678, SUN SIMAO, A PROMINENT DOCTOR OF THE TANG DYNASTY, CREATED ACUPUNCTURE CHARTS WHICH SHOWED THE MERIDIANS OF THE BODY.

SINCE THE TANG DYNASTY, ACUPUNCTURE AND MOXIBUSTION WERE REQUIRED FOR MEDICAL EDUCATION IN IMPERIAL CHINA.

I like to listen to Dr. Wang's lectures.

Yes, he's quite good. But I don't like the idea of practicing on myself!

Shh! Here he comes!

28

WANG WEIYI DREW UP PLANS FOR A LIFE SIZE MODEL.

Here is my proposal to cast bronze figures to be used for teaching acupuncture. Please give it to the Emperor.

Any news on my proposal, Sir?

His Majesty said that charts have been used since the ancient days. Why change?

Please, Sir. It would aid the students greatly.

Let me think about it.

Doctor Wang! Doctor Wang! Come quick!

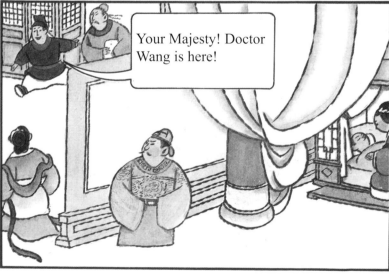

Your Majesty! Doctor Wang is here!

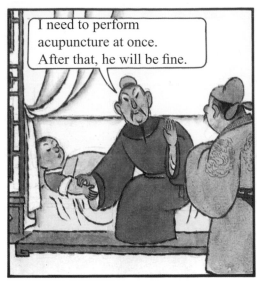

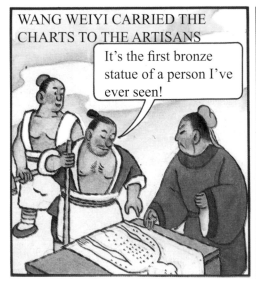

IN 1027, TWO BRONZE STATUES WERE CAST. THE STATUES ARE INSCRIBED WITH 666 POINTS FOR ACUPUNCTURE AND MOXIBUSTION, AND 259 ACUPOINTS ALONG THE 14 MERIDIAN SYSTEMS.

THE IMPERIAL MEDICAL INSTITUTE INTRODUCED A STRICT EXAMINATION SYSTEM TO PROMOTE ONLY THE MOST QUALIFIED DOCTORS.

32

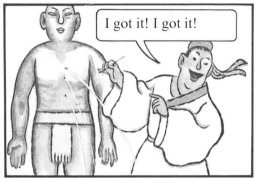

WANG COMPILED A MULTI-VOLUME BOOK ENTITLED *AN ILLUSTRATED MANUAL OF BRONZE FIGURE ACUPOINTS* WHICH QUICKLY BECAME THE MEDICAL STANDARD.

WANG WEIYI'S TEACHINGS WERE IMMORTALIZED ON A STONE TABLET WHICH ATTRACTED DISCIPLES FROM AFAR.

WANG WEIYI DEFINED THE TECHNIQUES OF ACUPUNCTURE DURING THE SONG DYNASTY.

LI SHIZHEN AND THE *MATERIA MEDICA*

李时珍

LI SHIZHEN (1518-1593) WAS A DISTINGUISHED DOCTOR OF THE MING DYNASTY. HE SPENT 27 YEARS COMPILING THE MOST COMPLETE GUIDE TO THE MEDICINES OF ANCIENT CHINA, KNOWN AS THE *COMPENDIUM OF MATERIA MEDICA*.

What's the matter?

My mother took a prescription he prepared but died soon afterwards!

Let me see the prescription.

Here.

This prescription is correct. Take me to your home to see the medicine.

The herbalist misused *gouwen* as *huangjing*! We must go there at once!

Here is the herbalist.

Doctor Li, if you read *this* description it clearly states that *gouwen* and *huangjing* are the same herbal medicines.

Now you read *this*. It is compendium of medicines of the Ming Dynasty. *Gouwen* is very toxic but *huangjing* is not. If you confuse the two...

But…

These two books have two ways of saying the same thing. I should not be blamed.

So whose fault is it that my mother died wrongly?!

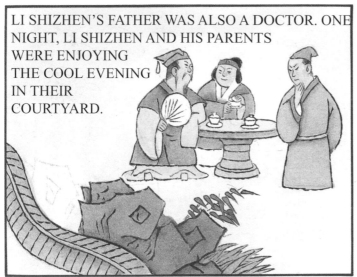

LI SHIZHEN'S FATHER WAS ALSO A DOCTOR. ONE NIGHT, LI SHIZHEN AND HIS PARENTS WERE ENJOYING THE COOL EVENING IN THEIR COURTYARD.

Are you still thinking about that poor man?

We have dozens of medical books at home in which many errors can be found. Why can't we write a new book?

Only the Imperial court could take on a project so large.

Doctor Li! Doctor Li Shizhen!

I've been sent by Duke Chu. You must come immediately. His son is gravely ill!

The prescription he was given is incorrect. He's fainted.

It's the dose that must be wrong!

This prescription can't be wrong!

Try this instead.

Here, get this prescription quickly.

Oh no! He's throwing up!

We have superior herbal medicines, but Li Shizhen prescribed some inferior medicine! What gall!

We must stop him at once!

Daddy!

The baby's thrown up everything he had in his stomach. He's fine now.

Doctor Li, you've saved my son! You shall be rewarded.

I humbly request that I be allowed to study in the Imperial Medical Institute.

I hereby command it!

IN 1556, LI SHIZHEN WAS APPOINTED CHIEF DIRECTOR OF THE IMPERIAL MEDICAL INSTITUTE. THERE HE GAINED KNOWLEDGE ABOUT ALL THE TYPES OF MEDICINES AND HERBAL REMEDIES IN THE IMPERIAL COLLECTION.

THE IMPERIAL MEDICAL INSTITUTE ALSO POSSESSED MEDICAL BOOKS FROM DYNASTIES PAST. LI SHIZHEN RESOLVED TO REVISE THE *MATERIA MEDICA*.

This book also lumps *huangjing* and *gouwen* together, which can do people great harm.

Look at the paragraph on *badou*: "A person will die after taking one *badou*, while a mouse will increase its weight by 50 grams." It's ridiculous!

Why doesn't the Imperial Medical Institute revise these texts?

They are all old-fashioned. Doctors in the Imperial Medical Institute only try to make immortality pills. No one is responsible for revising or checking the accuracy of old texts.

It must be left to me, then.

Write this: "Increase three times the amount of mercury and cinnabar, or the elixirs of life cannot be found."

Commissioner, the *materia medica* has not been revised in several hundred years. The old texts have too many mistakes. I humbly ask that we revise them.

We don't have enough resources to refine the pills of immortality. How can we possibly undertake the task of revising the medical texts?

You're just an herbalist!

39

Li Shizhen! You only know low-grade herbal medicines. You should refine your techniques of immortality pill-making!

Mercury and cinnabar are poisonous! How can they be made into pills of immortality?

Hold your tongue! You attempt to change the classics and slander the alchemists? Your suggestions cannot be authorized.

LI SHIZHEN WAS SO ANGRY THAT HE RESIGNED FROM HIS POST AND RETURNED TO HIS HOMETOWN.

UNFORTUNATELY, LI SHIZHEN'S FATHER HAD DIED SUDDENLY.

Here are the books your father wanted you to have.

Father, I have decided to revise the compendium of *Materia Medica*.

40

PEOPLE SUBMITTED THEIR PRESCRIPTIONS TO DR. LI.

LI SHIZHEN CHECKED, ARRANGED, AND CATEGORIZED THE PRESCRIPTIONS AND HERBAL MEDICINES.

IN 1565, LI SHIZHEN, STILL WITH INNUMERABLE QUESTIONS ON HIS MIND ABOUT THE ANCIENT *MATERIA MEDICA*, STARTED A TEN-YEAR EXPEDITION.

Can you throw down a stem of *noble dendrobium*!

Here it comes!

Sir, do you know of the herbal medicine called *zhiyuan*?

Of course. There are big and small-leaf varieties. Each has different properties. The small-leaf *zhiyuan* grows over there.

Write down whatever he says quickly. This is contradictory to what scholars have recorded in dynasties past.

Look how steep it is!

AFTER SEVERAL MONTHS THEY ARRIVED AT WUDANG MOUNTAIN.

It is said that plums on Wudang Mountain will give you immortality. Is it true?

We won't find out unless we try one!

Let's ask that woodsman.

Excuse me. Where are the plum trees?

There are several plum treets at Jiulong Palace. It is said that the plums are very precious. One can live a long time after eating them.

The plum trees are over there.

I see.

My! It's sour!

If you eat more, you'll become immortal!

It promotes the secretion of saliva and therefore quenches your thirst.

Why is everyone so animated?

The Emperor is dead! It is said that he died after taking the immortality pills. All the alchemists were beheaded!

My revision of the *materia medica* will correct the harmful prescriptions and remove the witch-doctor remedies.

Where is the manager?

He went to Yaowang Temple in Nanjing. Right now there is a gathering of all kinds of herbalists going on there.

This is our chance. Let's go to Nanjing!

OK!

This is wonderful! Look at all the herbal medicines available!

You two remember the properties and draw sketches of as many medicines as you can. Be careful not to make any mistakes.

What's this medicine? I've never seen anything like this before.

It's called *sanqi*. It helps stop bleeding and eases pain.

If a woman bleeds after having a baby, she can take it. It has a curative effect.

Another new medicine! Let me have a small amount please.

Right away.

Uh oh! That's the last of our money.

It's OK. Give it to me.

It's good that we ran out of money so we can go home now.

THEY HAD JOURNEYED THOUSANDS OF MILES AND HAD AMASSED ENOUGH INFORMATION TO COMPLETE THEIR REVISIONS. FINALLY THEY ARRIVED HOME.

Beginning tomorrow, we will begin to compile the book.

I want to help too!

Doctor Li, which category does this belong to?

Mineral.

LI SHIZHEN DIVIDED HIS DATA INTO 16 PARTS AND 62 CATEGORIES ACCORDING TO PLANT, ANIMAL, AND MINERAL. THIS WAS A DEPARTURE FROM THE EXISTING GRADES OF HERBAL MEDICINES, NAMELY, SUPERIOR, MIDDLE, AND INFERIOR. LI SHIZHEN'S METHOD WAS SURPRISINGLY SIMILAR TO THAT OF CONTEMPORARY SCIENTIFIC CLASSIFICATION PRINCIPLES.

LI SHIZHEN WROTE DOWN IN DETAIL THE NAME, GEOGRAPHIC LOCATION, SHAPE, METHOD OF CULTIVATION, AND COLLECTION INFORMATION OF EACH TYPE OF HERBAL MEDICINE ALONG WITH A SKETCH.

AFTER 27 YEARS OF HARD WORK, LI SHIZHEN, AT THE AGE OF 61, COMPLETED THE MONUMENTAL WORK ENTITLED *COMPENDIUM OF MATERIA MEDICA*.

LI SHIZHEN DIED IN 1593 AT THE AGE OF 75.

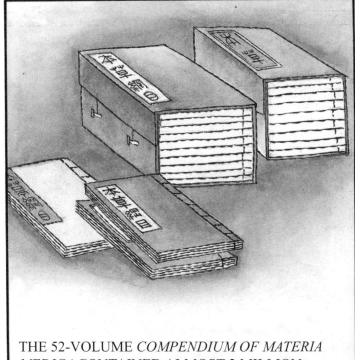

THE 52-VOLUME *COMPENDIUM OF MATERIA MEDICA* CONTAINED ALMOST 2 MILLION CHINESE CHARACTERS, AND FEATURED DESCRIPTIONS OF 1,892 MEDICINES, WITH 1,160 ILLUSTRATIONS AND 11,096 PRESCRIPTIONS.

IN 1596, THREE YEARS AFTER LI'S DEATH, THE COMPENDIUM WAS PUBLISHED AND RELEASED TO DOCTORS AND SCHOLARS. IT BECAME A CLASSIC WORK OF TRADITIONAL CHINESE MEDICINE AND HAS INFLUENCED COUNTLESS STUDENTS OF CHINESE MEDICINE THROUGH THE CENTURIES. IT HAS SINCE BEEN TRANSLATED INTO MANY LANGUAGES AND SOLD THROUGHOUT THE WORLD.

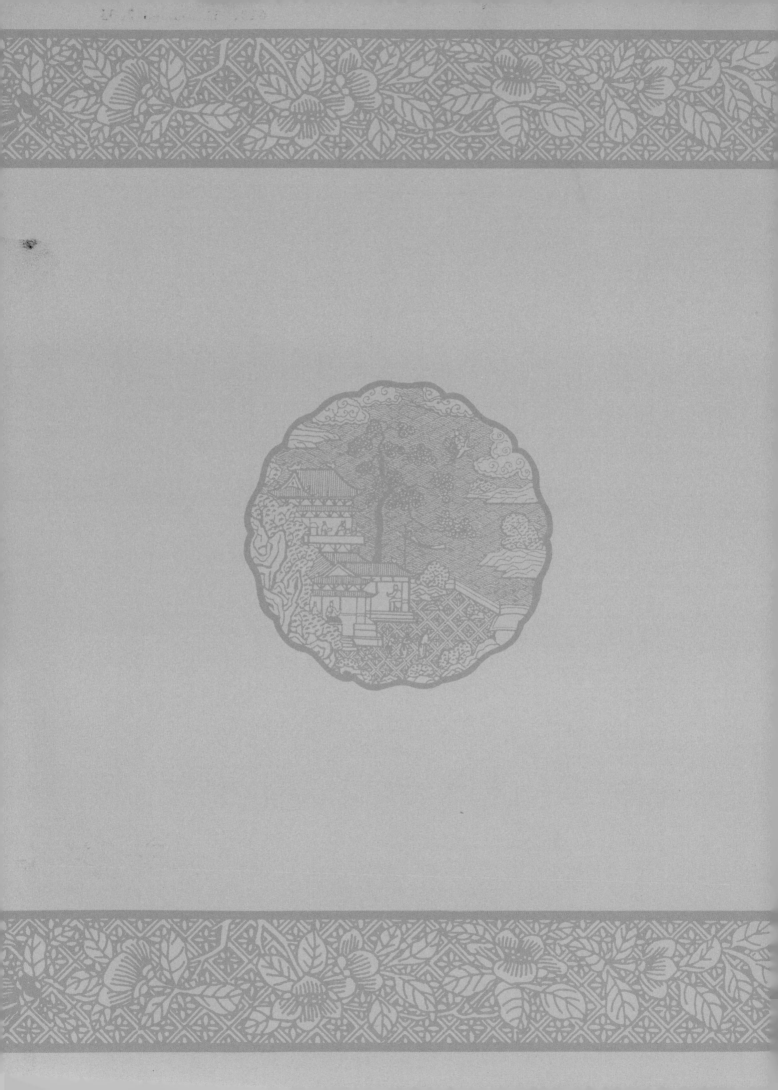